CHEER UP

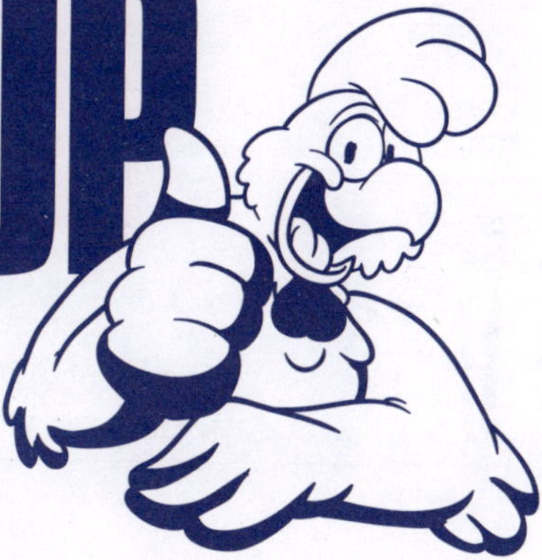

Published 2024

FiNGERPRINT!

An imprint of Prakash Books India Pvt. Ltd

113/A, Darya Ganj,
New Delhi-110 002
Email: info@prakashbooks.com/sales@prakashbooks.com

 Fingerprint Publishing
 @FingerprintP
 @fingerprintpublishingbooks
www.fingerprintpublishing.com

ISBN: 978 93 5856 684 0

To....................

From....................

Keeping that smile on our faces when everything is going downhill is a challenge we all face.

But we cannot frown our way through life now, can we?

Challenges are defined by our response to them, and nothing can shake a cheerful heart! Once we learn to cheer up ourselves and others around us, we will sail through the turbulent waters of life.

So, amid the days of doom and gloom, remember to Cheer Up!

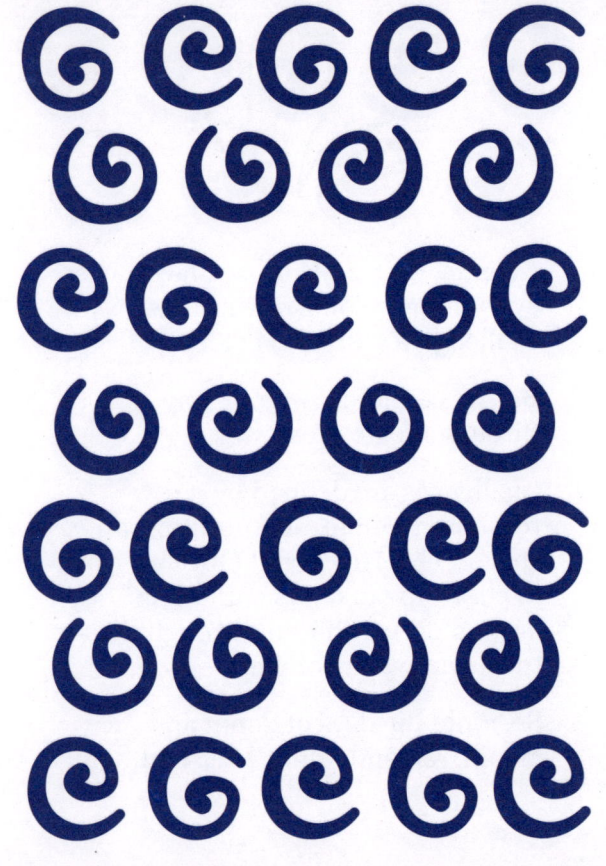

"YOU FIND YOURSELF REFRESHED IN THE PRESENCE OF CHEERFUL PEOPLE. WHY NOT MAKE AN HONEST EFFORT TO CONFER THAT PLEASURE ON OTHERS?"

Lydia M. Child

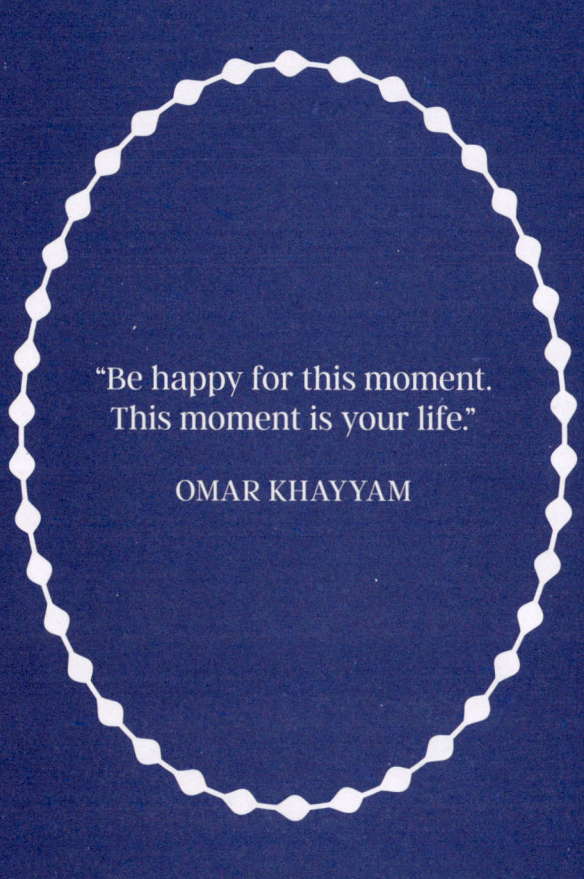

"Be happy for this moment.
This moment is your life."

OMAR KHAYYAM

"IT'S BETTER TO HAVE LOVED
AND LOST THAN NEVER
TO HAVE LOVED AT ALL."

Alfred, Lord Tennyson

"In the dance of life, sometimes we stumble, but it's in the rhythm of resilience that we find the strength to turn missteps into moments of joy."

BRENE BROWN

"Pessimism leads to weakness,
optimism to power."

WILLIAM JAMES

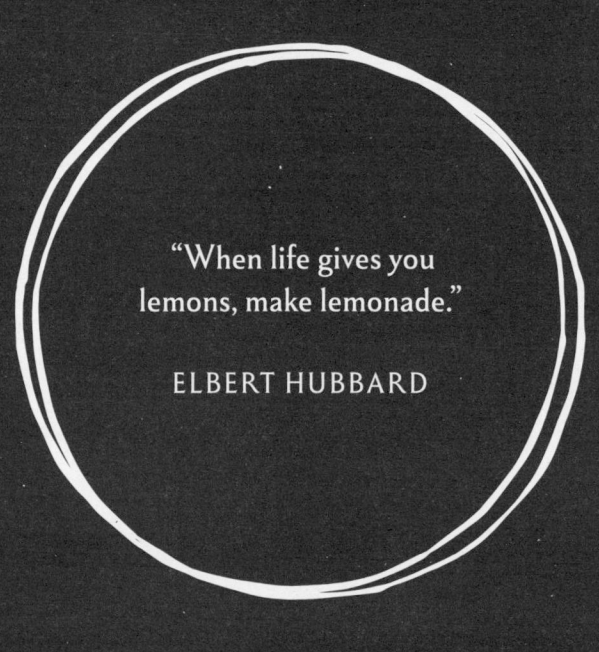

"When life gives you
lemons, make lemonade."

ELBERT HUBBARD

"IF MORE OF US VALUED FOOD
AND CHEER AND SONG ABOVE
HOARDED GOLD, IT WOULD
BE A MERRIER WORLD."

J. R. R. Tolkien

"I am determined to be cheerful and happy in whatever situation I may find myself. For I have learned that the greater part of our misery or unhappiness is determined not by our circumstance but by our disposition."

MARTHA WASHINGTON

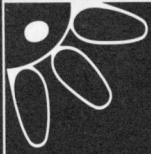
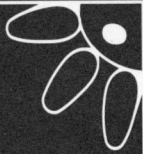

"The best way to cheer
yourself up is to try to
cheer somebody else up."

MARK TWAIN

"THE MAN WHO RADIATES GOOD CHEER, WHO MAKES LIFE HAPPIER WHEREVER HE MEETS IT, IS ALWAYS A MAN OF VISION AND FAITH."

Ella Wheeler Wilcox

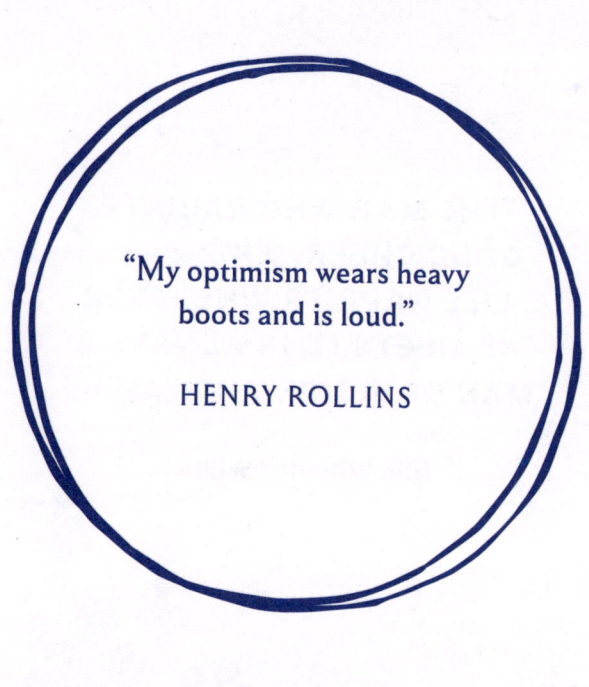

"My optimism wears heavy boots and is loud."

HENRY ROLLINS

"I hope you know what a brave,
important, sparkling,
and wonderful human you always
are, even if you don't speak like it."

ANONYMOUS

"Don't take things too seriously, and just chill."

ANONYMOUS

"Life is really simple,
but we insist on making
it complicated."

CONFUCIUS

"I believe that God
put us in this jolly world
to be happy and enjoy life."

ROBERT BADEN-POWELL

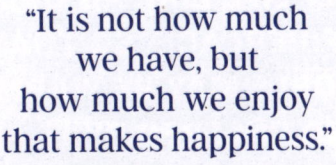

"It is not how much
we have, but
how much we enjoy
that makes happiness."

CHARLES SPURGEON

"I SAY TO MYSELF THAT I SHALL TRY TO MAKE MY LIFE LIKE AN OPEN FIREPLACE, SO THAT PEOPLE MAY BE WARMED AND CHEERED BY IT AND SO GO OUT THEMSELVES TO WARM AND CHEER."

George Matthew Adams

"The best of healers is good cheer."

PINDAR

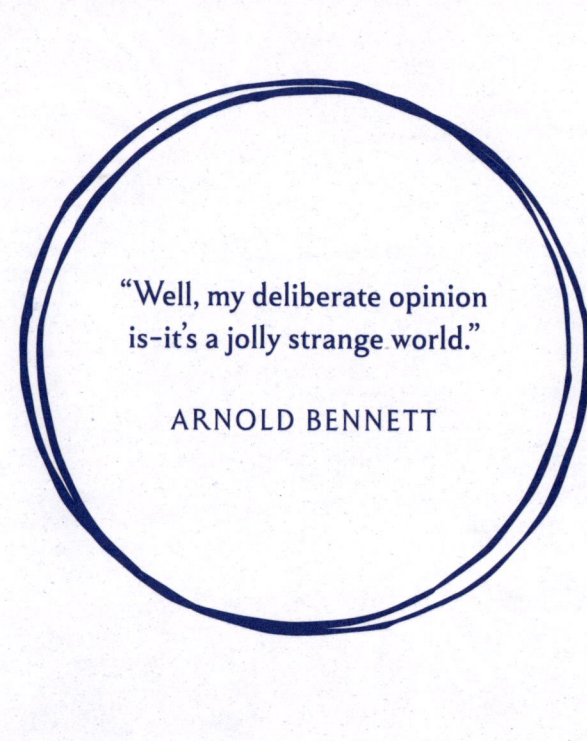

"Well, my deliberate opinion
is–it's a jolly strange world."

ARNOLD BENNETT

"NEVER, EVER UNDERESTIMATE THE IMPORTANCE OF HAVING FUN."

Randy Pausch

"Winning is only half of it.
Having fun is the other half."

BUM PHILLIPS

"IF A MAN INSISTED ALWAYS
ON BEING SERIOUS, AND NEVER
ALLOWED HIMSELF A BIT OF FUN
AND RELAXATION, HE WOULD
GO MAD OR BECOME UNSTABLE
WITHOUT KNOWING IT."

Herodotus

"LIFE IS TOUGH,
MY DARLING,
BUT SO ARE YOU."

Stephanie Bennett-Henry

"There is always someone better off than you, and there is always someone worse off than you."

C.L. HALL

"You'll never find a rainbow
if you're looking down."

CHARLIE CHAPLIN

"Cheerfulness is the very flower of health."

CHINESE PROVERB

"A SMILE IS THE
UNIVERSAL WELCOME."

Max Eastman

"I've never met a strong
person with an easy past."

ANONYMOUS

"Be of good cheer.
The future is as
bright as your faith."

THOMAS S MONSON

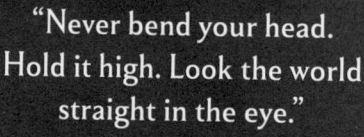

"Never bend your head.
Hold it high. Look the world
straight in the eye."

HELEN KELLER

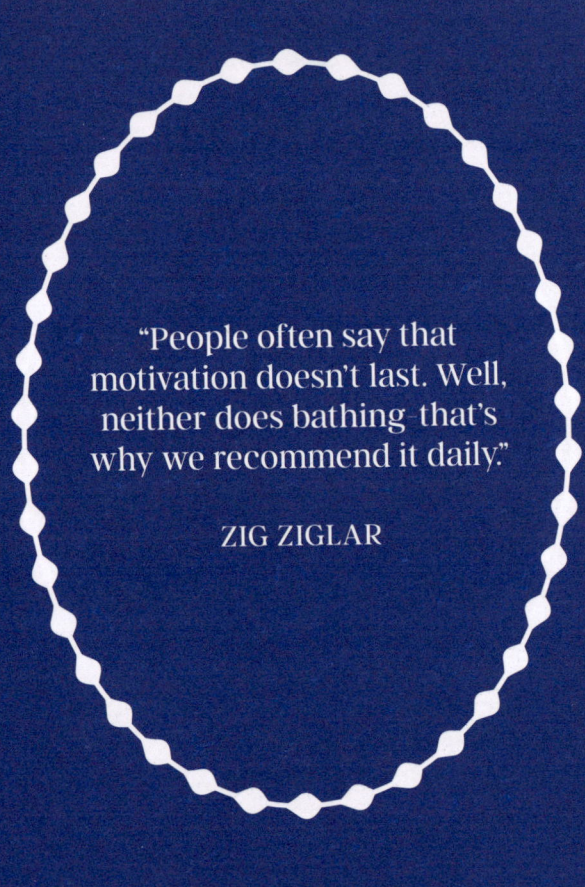

"People often say that motivation doesn't last. Well, neither does bathing—that's why we recommend it daily."

ZIG ZIGLAR

"FIND A PLACE INSIDE WHERE THERE'S JOY, AND THE JOY WILL BURN OUT THE PAIN."

Joseph Campbell

"I SLEPT AND DREAMT THAT
LIFE WAS JOY. I AWOKE AND
SAW THAT LIFE WAS SERVICE.
I ACTED AND BEHOLD,
SERVICE WAS JOY."

Rabindranath Tagore

HOW TO CHEER UP
WHEN YOU ARE FEELING DOWN?

- Start your day with a smile!

- Call your loved ones! Sometimes, having a nice chat with your family or friends is all you need.

- Count your blessings! Be grateful for what you have. Often, in our pursuit of things, we neglect the little things that bring us happiness.

- Treat yourself. Take yourself out to your favourite restaurant or simply enjoy your favourite ice cream!

- Listen to music! Music has the power to heal and is a sure-shot way to improve your mood.

- Write down your feelings. You may never know, but it might give you the clarity you need about your emotions.

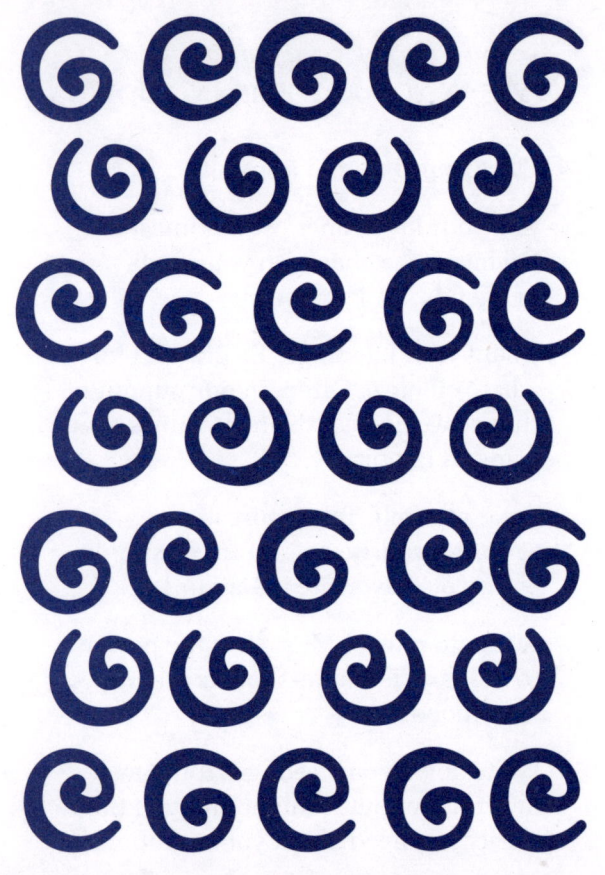

"A SMILE IS A CURVE THAT SETS
EVERYTHING STRAIGHT."

Phyllis Diller

"Smile, it's free therapy."

DOUGLAS HORTON

"After every storm the sun
will smile; for every problem
there is a solution, and
the soul's indefeasible duty
is to be of good cheer."

WILLIAM R. ALGER

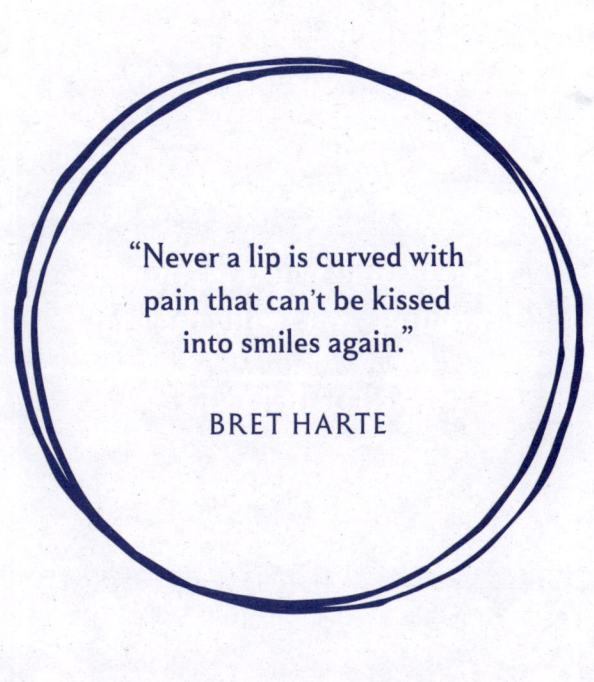

"Never a lip is curved with pain that can't be kissed into smiles again."

BRET HARTE

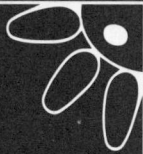

"If you smile when no one else
is around, you really mean it."

ANDY ROONEY

"REAL MEN LAUGH AT OPPOSITION; REAL MEN SMILE WHEN ENEMIES APPEAR."

Marcus Garvey

"THE PERSON WHO CAN BRING
THE SPIRIT OF LAUGHTER INTO
A ROOM IS INDEED BLESSED."

Bennett Cerf

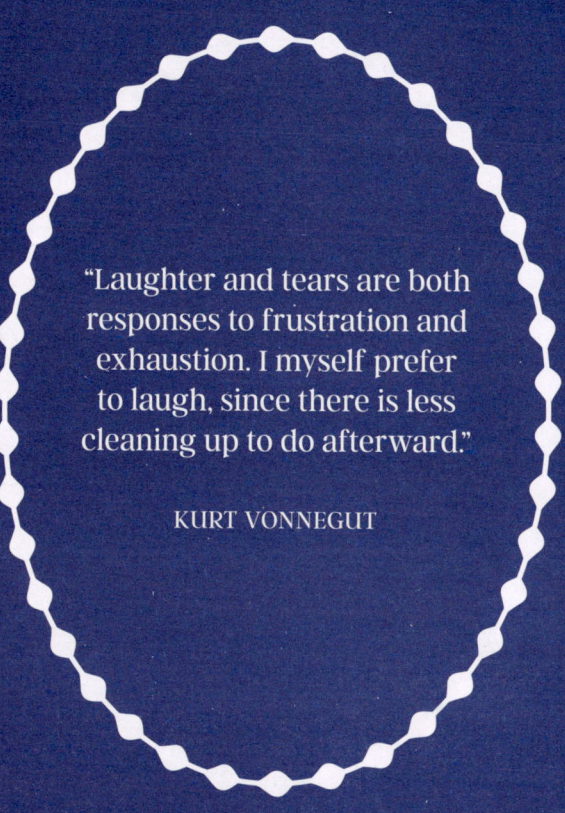

"Laughter and tears are both
responses to frustration and
exhaustion. I myself prefer
to laugh, since there is less
cleaning up to do afterward."

KURT VONNEGUT

"LAUGHTER IS THE SUN THAT DRIVES WINTER FROM THE HUMAN FACE."

Victor Hugo

"Being happy doesn't mean that everything is perfect. It simply means that you've decided to look beyond the imperfections of life."

ANONYMOUS

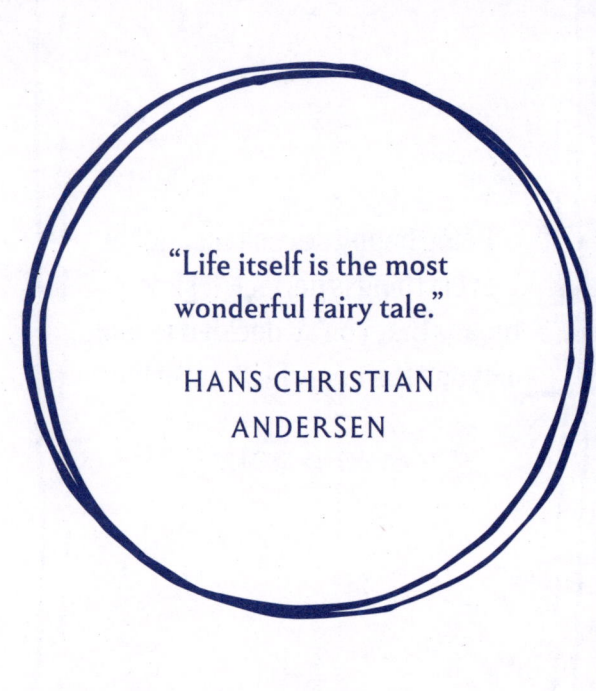

"Life itself is the most
wonderful fairy tale."

HANS CHRISTIAN
ANDERSEN

"Life isn't a matter of milestones,
but of moments."

ROSE KENNEDY

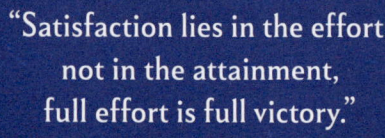

"Satisfaction lies in the effort,
not in the attainment,
full effort is full victory."

MAHATMA GANDHI

"HAPPINESS DOES NOT COME FROM DOING EASY WORK BUT FROM THE AFTERGLOW OF SATISFACTION THAT COMES AFTER THE ACHIEVEMENT OF A DIFFICULT TASK THAT DEMANDED OUR BEST."

Theodore Isaac Rubin

"If you're going through hell,
keep going."

WINSTON CHURCHILL

"Faith is the bird that feels the light
when the dawn is still dark."

RABINDRANATH TAGORE

"CHEERFULNESS IS
THE BEST PROMOTER
OF HEALTH AND IS AS
FRIENDLY TO THE MIND
AS TO THE BODY."

JOSEPH ADDISON

"YOUR ATTITUDE IS LIKE A BOX OF CRAYONS THAT COLOR YOUR WORLD."

Allen Klein

"The greatest self is a peaceful smile, that always sees the world smiling back."

BRYANT H. MCGILL

"NEVER, NEVER, NEVER
GIVE UP YOUR SMILE."

Anonymous

"LAUGHTER IS THE SOUND
OF THE SOUL DANCING."

Jarod Kintz

"A pessimist sees the difficulty
in every opportunity;
an optimist sees the
opportunity in every difficulty."

WINSTON CHURCHILL

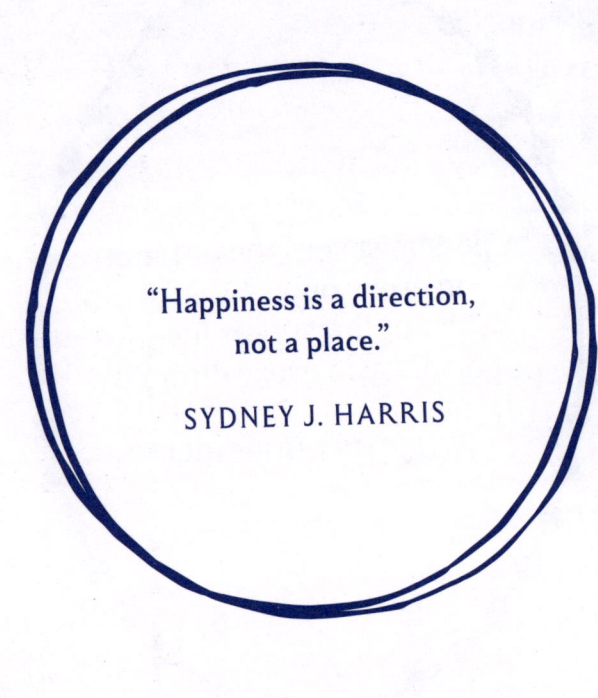

"Happiness is a direction,
not a place."

SYDNEY J. HARRIS

"In this hour, I do not believe
that any darkness will endure."

J.R.R. TOLKIEN

"Happiness is an inside job."

WILLIAM ARTHUR WARD

"Cheerfulness, it would appear,
is a matter which depends fully as much
on the state of things within, as on the
state of things without and around us."

CHARLOTTE BRONTE

"NOTHING ELSE IN ALL
LIFE IS SUCH A MAKER
OF JOY AND CHEER AS THE
PRIVILEGE OF DOING GOOD."

J.R. Miller

"WHEN EVERYTHING FEELS
LIKE AN UPHILL STRUGGLE
JUST THINK OF THE VIEW
FROM THE TOP."

Anonymous

"Everything you can
imagine is real."

PABLO PICASSO

"CHEERFULNESS IS THE
ATMOSPHERE IN WHICH
ALL THINGS THRIVE."

Jean Paul Richter

"Amidst the storms of life, remember, you are the captain of your own ship. Weather the waves, adjust your sails, and let the winds of hope guide you to calmer seas."

SARAH BAN BREATHNACH

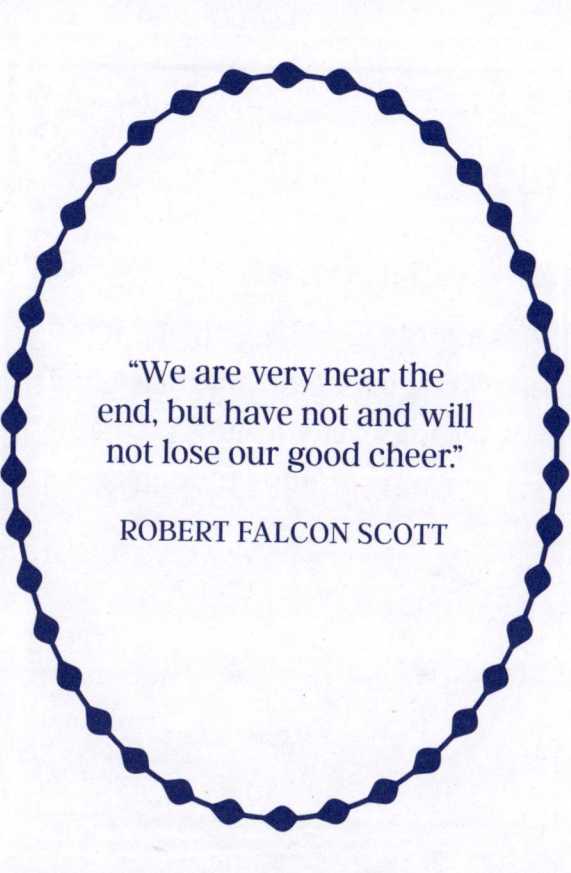

"We are very near the
end, but have not and will
not lose our good cheer."

ROBERT FALCON SCOTT

"Into each life some rain must fall."

HENRY WADSWORTH
LONGFELLOW

"If you look the right way,
you can see that the whole
world is a garden."

FRANCES HODGSON
BURNETT

"Let us be of cheer, remembering
that the misfortunes hardest to
bear are those which never come."

JAMES RUSSELL LOWELL

"LAUGHTER IS THE BRUSH
THAT SWEEPS AWAY THE
COBWEBS OF THE HEART."

Mort Walker

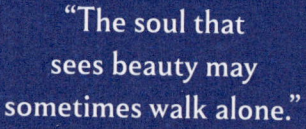

"The soul that
sees beauty may
sometimes walk alone."

OHANN WOLFGANG
VON GOETHE

"IN THE CENTRAL PLACE
OF EVERY HEART, THERE
IS A RECORDING CHAMBER;
SO LONG AS IT RECEIVES
MESSAGES OF BEAUTY, HOPE,
CHEER AND COURAGE,
YOU ARE YOUNG."

Samuel Ullman

"Life is not a problem to be solved,
but a reality to be experienced."

SØREN KIERKEGAARD

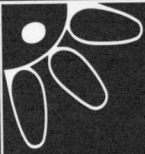
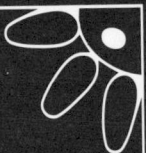

"We can complain because rose bushes have thorns, or rejoice because thorns have roses."

ALPHONSE KARR

"WHEN ONE DOOR OF HAPPINESS
CLOSES, ANOTHER OPENS,
BUT OFTEN WE LOOK SO LONG
AT THE CLOSED DOOR THAT
WE DO NOT SEE THE ONE THAT
HAS BEEN OPENED FOR US."

Helen Keller

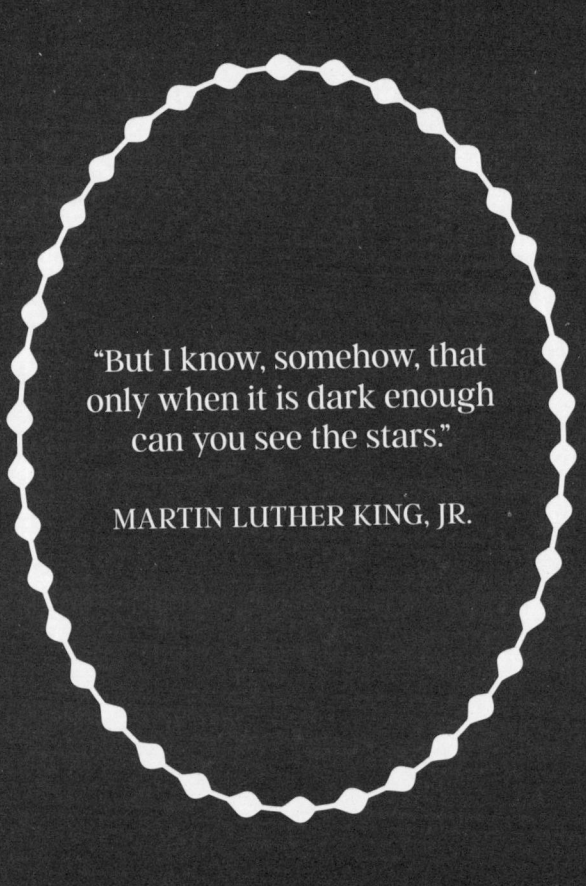

"But I know, somehow, that only when it is dark enough can you see the stars."

MARTIN LUTHER KING, JR.

"Very little is needed to make a happy life; it is all within yourself, in your way of thinking."

MARCUS AURELIUS

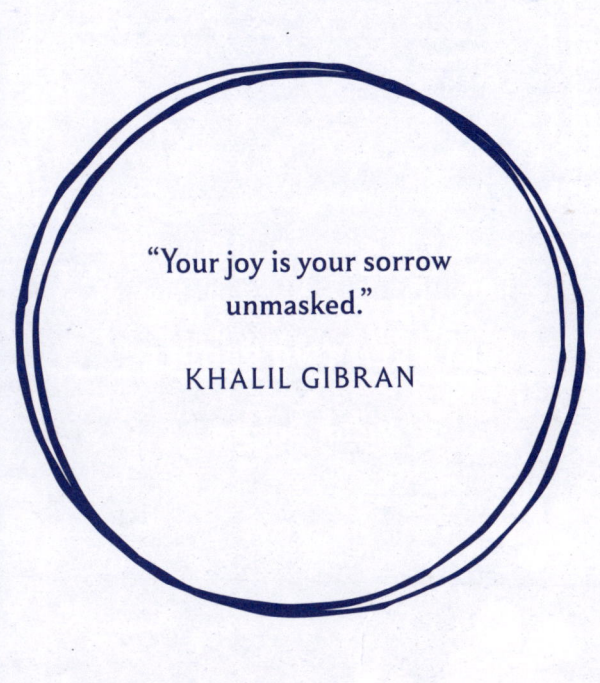

"Your joy is your sorrow
unmasked."

KHALIL GIBRAN

"LAUGHTER IS THE SHORTEST DISTANCE BETWEEN TWO PEOPLE."

Victor Borge

"With the new day comes new strength and new thoughts."

ELEANOR ROOSEVELT

"People deal too much with the
negative, with what is wrong.
Why not try and see positive things,
to just touch those things and
make them bloom?"

THICH NHAT HANH

"Every society needs people who can encourage and stimulate and cheer. They are the ones who make the world run. You can be one of them!"

RICHARD M. DEVOS

"A GOOD LAUGH IS SUNSHINE IN THE HOUSE."

William Makepeace Thackeray

"Few things in the world are more powerful than a positive push. A smile. A world of optimism and hope. A 'you can do it' when things are tough."

RICHARD M. DEVOS

"The more the panic grows, the more uplifting the image of a man who refuses to bow to the terror."

ERNST JUNGER

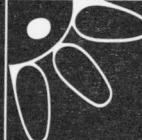

"The world is indeed full
of peril, and in it, there are
many dark places; but still,
there is much that is fair, and
though in all lands love is now
mingled with grief, it grows
perhaps the greater."

J.R.R. TOLKIEN

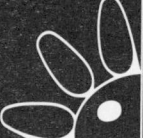

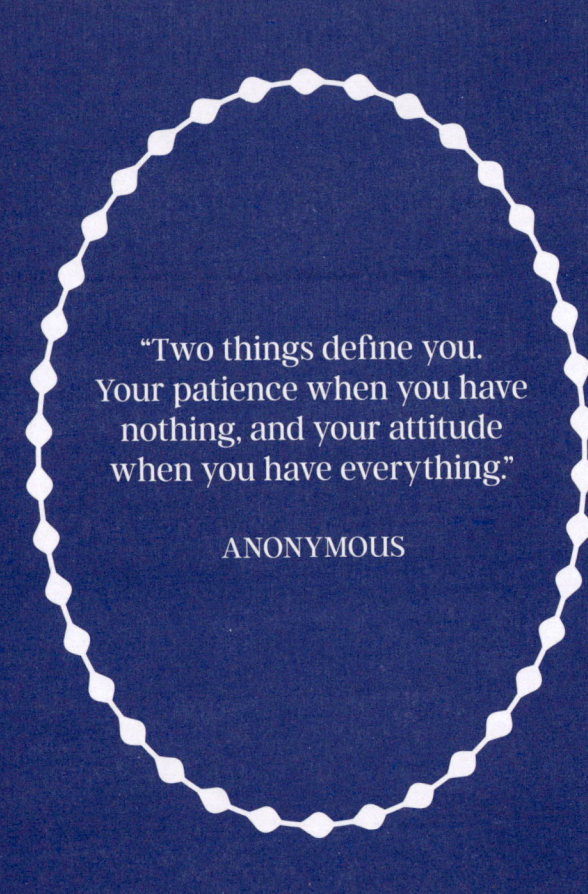

"Two things define you.
Your patience when you have
nothing, and your attitude
when you have everything."

ANONYMOUS

"THERE IS A CRACK IN EVERYTHING. THAT'S HOW THE LIGHT GETS IN."

Leonard Cohen

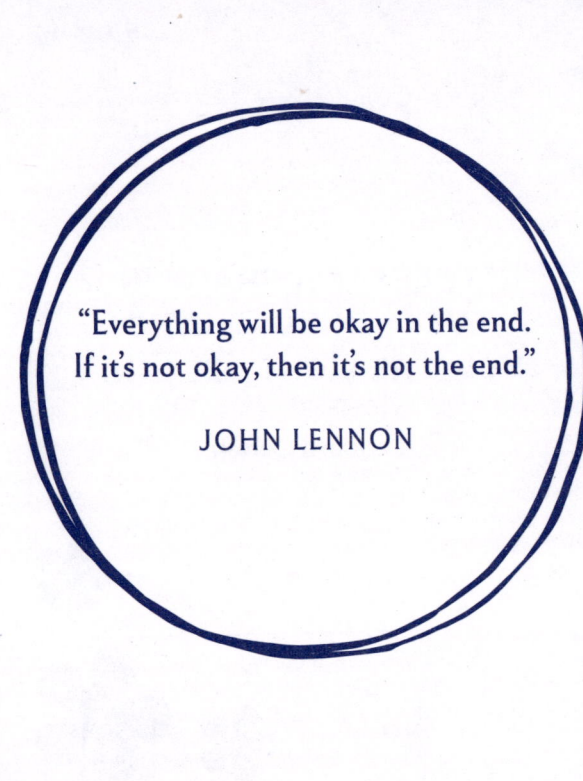

"Everything will be okay in the end.
If it's not okay, then it's not the end."

JOHN LENNON

"You'll find that life is still worthwhile if you just smile."

CHARLIE CHAPLIN

"Each age has deemed the new-born year the fittest time for festal cheer."

SIR WALTER SCOTT

"AND FROM THE MIDST
OF CHEERLESS GLOOM
I PASSED TO BRIGHT
UNCLOUDED DAY."

Emily Bronte

"A poet is a nightingale, who sits in darkness and sings to cheer its own solitude with sweet sounds."

PERCY BYSSHE SHELLEY

"We speak much of the duty
of making others happy.
No day should pass, we say,
on which we do not put a little
cheer into some discouraged
heart, make the path a little
smoother for someone's tired
feet, or help some fainting
robin unto its nest again."

J.R. MILLER

"NO MATTER WHAT LOOMS AHEAD, IF YOU CAN EAT TODAY, ENJOY TODAY, MIX GOOD CHEER WITH FRIENDS TODAY, ENJOY IT AND BLESS GOD FOR IT."

Henry Ward Beecher

"Don't worry if you had a bad day, remember there are people who have their ex's name tattooed on their body."

ANONYMOUS

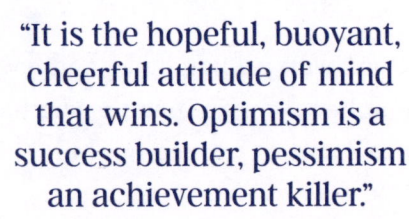

"It is the hopeful, buoyant, cheerful attitude of mind that wins. Optimism is a success builder, pessimism an achievement killer."

ORISON SWETT MARDEN

"THE MOST CERTAIN SIGN OF
WISDOM IS CHEERFULNESS."

Michel de Montaigne

"Cheerfulness and contentment are great beautifiers, and are famous preservers of good looks."

CHARLES DICKENS

"And so of cheerfulness, or a good temper—the more it is spent, the more of it remains."

RALPH WALDO EMERSON

"FOR THERE IS NO FRIEND LIKE
A SISTER IN CALM OR STORMY
WEATHER; TO CHEER ONE ON
THE TEDIOUS WAY, TO FETCH
ONE IF ONE GOES ASTRAY,
TO LIFT ONE IF ONE TOTTERS
DOWN, TO STRENGTHEN
WHILST ONE STANDS."

Christina Rossetti

"Be cheerful—the problems that worry us most are those that never arrive."

BENJAMIN FRANKLIN

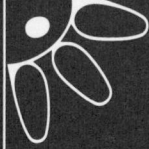

"The world would
rather see hope than just
hear its song. And that's why
statesman have to smile."

WISŁAWA SZYMBORSKA

"It is one life whether we spend
it laughing or weeping."

ANONYMOUS

"The greatest prayer you could ever pray is to laugh every day."

RAMTHA

LITTLE THINGS THAT MIGHT CHEER YOU UP

- Trees are friends and often communicate with one another.

- While taking a nap, sea-otters hold hands so that they do not drift apart in the water.

- Bats sing love songs to each other.

- Cats bring humans "presents" because they think we can't hunt for ourselves.

- Getting hugs and taking naps make you more productive.

- Happiness is actually contagious!

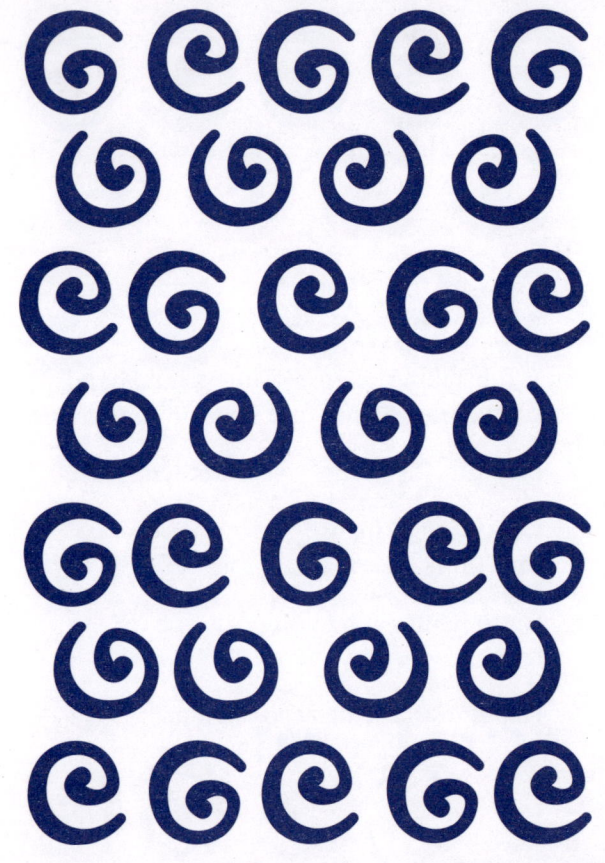

"Cheerfulness is a very great help in fostering the virtue of charity."

MOTHER TERESA

"CHEERFULNESS IN MOST CHEERFUL PEOPLE IS THE RICH AND SATISFYING RESULT OF STRENUOUS DISCIPLINE."

William Ellery Channing

"I ALWAYS CHEER UP IMMENSELY IF AN ATTACK IS PARTICULARLY WOUNDING BECAUSE I THINK, WELL, IF THEY ATTACK ONE PERSONALLY, IT MEANS THEY HAVE NOT A SINGLE POLITICAL ARGUMENT LEFT."

Margaret Thatcher

"Laughter is an instant vacation."

MILTON BERLE

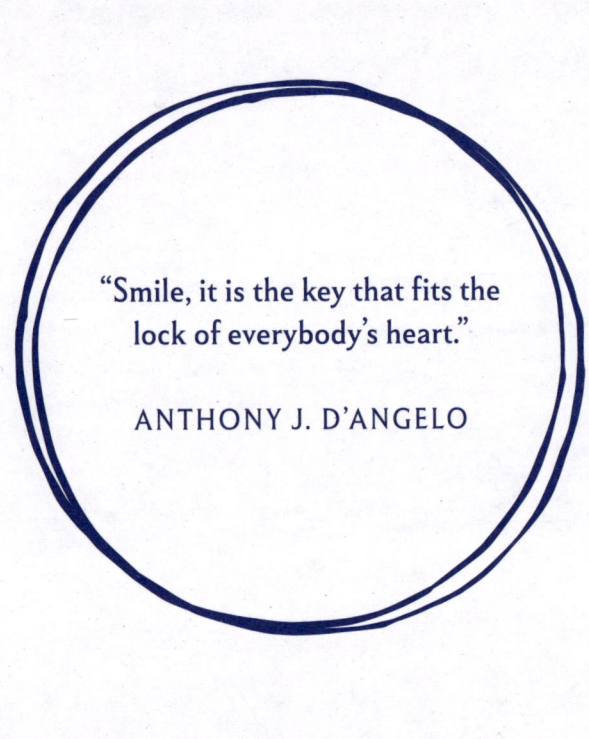

"Smile, it is the key that fits the
lock of everybody's heart."

ANTHONY J. D'ANGELO

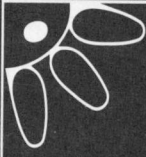
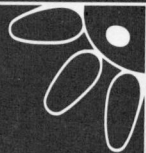

"Difficulties in life are intended
to make us better, not bitter."

DAN REEVES

"The best thing about
the future is that it comes
one day at a time."

ABRAHAM LINCOLN

"YOU'RE BRAVER THAN
YOU BELIEVE AND
STRONGER THAN YOU
SEEM, AND SMARTER
THAN YOU THINK."

A. A. Milne

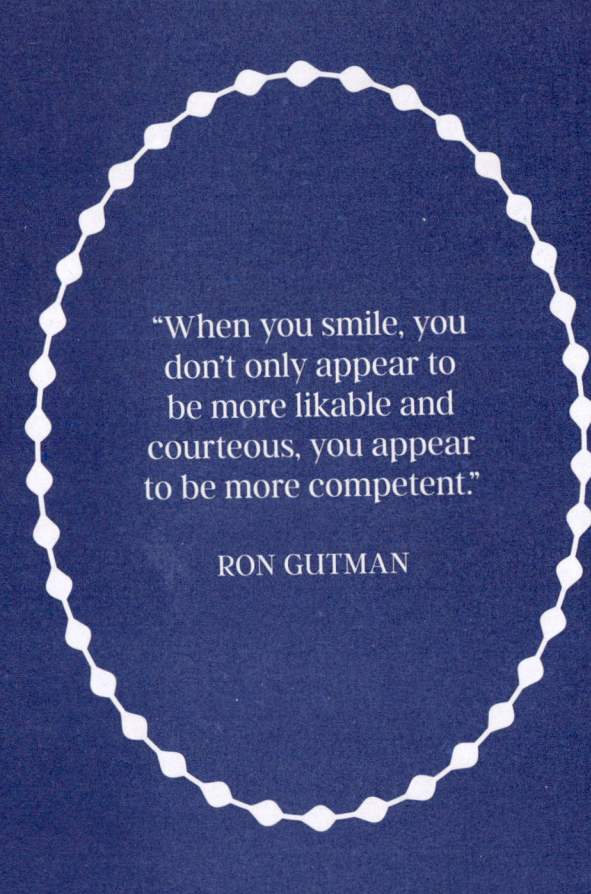

"When you smile, you don't only appear to be more likable and courteous, you appear to be more competent."

RON GUTMAN

"I'd far rather be happy
than right any day."

DOUGLAS ADAMS

"You can't be unhappy in the middle of a big, beautiful river."

JIM HARRISON

"By all these lovely tokens, September days are here, with summer's best of weather, and autumn's best of cheer."

HELEN HUNT JACKSON

"Do not take life too seriously.
You will never get out of it alive."

ELBERT HUBBARD

"May the forces of evil
become confused on the
way to your house."

GEORGE CARLIN

"ONE ADVANTAGE TO
TALKING TO YOURSELF IS
THAT YOU KNOW AT LEAST
SOMEBODY'S LISTENING."

Franklin P. Jones

"If you think nobody cares if you're alive, try missing a couple of car payments."

EARL WILSON

"The best way
to pay for a
lovely moment
is to enjoy it."

RICHARD BACH

"I'm sick of following my dreams, man. I'm just going to ask where they're going and hook up with 'em later."

MITCH HEDBERG

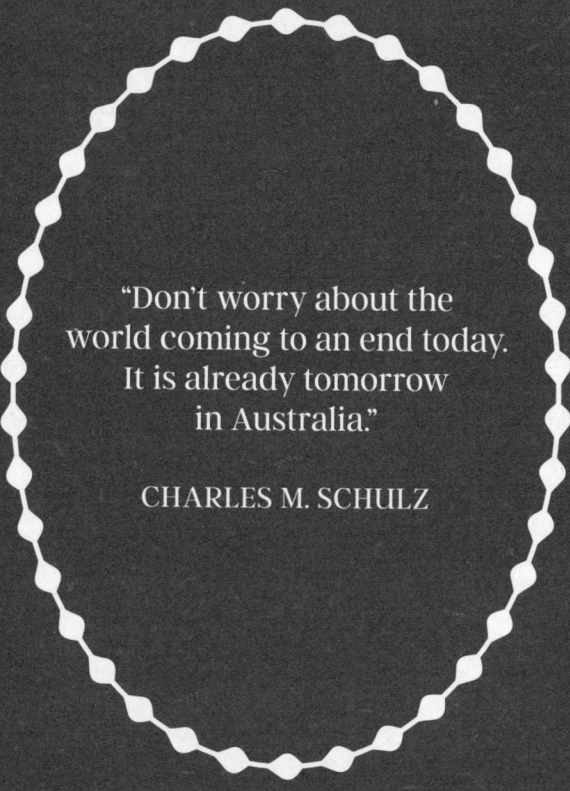

"Don't worry about the
world coming to an end today.
It is already tomorrow
in Australia."

CHARLES M. SCHULZ

"IF 'PLAN A' DIDN'T WORK.
THE ALPHABET HAS 25 MORE
LETTERS! STAY COOL."

Anonymous

"A diamond is merely a lump of coal that did well under pressure."

BEN ORCHARD

"THE DARKEST HOUR HAS ONLY SIXTY MINUTES."

Morris Mandel

"Every day may not be good,
but there's something
good in every day."

ALICE MORSE EARLE

"LAUGHTER IS A TRANQUILIZER WITH NO SIDE EFFECTS."

Arnold H. Glasow

"Wake up feeling exceptional.
You are important, needed,
and unique."

ANONYMOUS

"Don't let the negativity of the world get you down."

GERMANY KENT

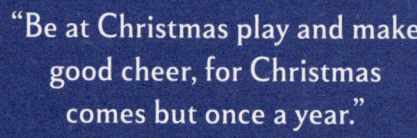

"Be at Christmas play and make good cheer, for Christmas comes but once a year."

THOMAS TUSSER

"A SMILE IS HAPPINESS YOU'LL FIND RIGHT UNDER YOUR NOSE."

Tom Wilson

"Everything has beauty,
but not everyone sees it."

CONFUCIUS

"Joy is not in things;
it is in us."

RICHARD WAGNER

"WHENEVER YOU FEEL SAD JUST REMEMBER THAT THERE ARE BILLIONS OF CELLS IN YOUR BODY AND ALL THEY CARE ABOUT IS YOU."

Anonymous

"THE ART OF BEING HAPPY
LIES IN THE POWER OF
EXTRACTING HAPPINESS
FROM COMMON THINGS."

Henry Ward Beecher

"The time when there is no one there
to feel sorry for you or to cheer for
you is when a player is made."

TIM DUNCAN

**"DO NOT GRIEVE.
ANYTHING YOU LOSE
COMES ROUND
IN ANOTHER FORM."**

Rumi

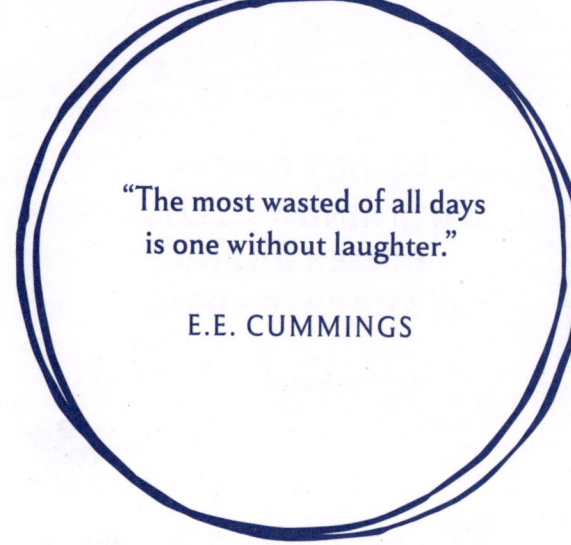

"The most wasted of all days
is one without laughter."

E.E. CUMMINGS

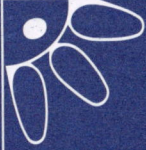

"Happiness is not something
ready-made. It comes from
your own actions."

14TH DALAI LAMA

"Life is 10% what happens
to us and 90% how we
react to it."

CHARLES R. SWINDOLL

"Success is not the key to happiness. Happiness is the key to success. If you love what you are doing, you will be successful."

ALBERT SCHWEITZER

"HAPPINESS IS A CHOICE.
CHOOSE TO SMILE AND
LET YOUR CHEERFULNESS
RADIATE TO THE WORLD."

Roy T. Bennett